Remarkable Landmarks

Our Grand Canyon

by Jennifer Prior, Ph.D.

Consultant
Cheryl Lane, M.Ed.
Classroom Teacher, California

Publishing Credits
Rachelle Cracchiolo, M.S.Ed., *Publisher*
Emily R. Smith, M.A.Ed., *SVP of Content Development*
Véronique Bos, *VP of Creative*
Dona Rice, *Senior Content Manager*
Dani Neiley, *Editor*
Fabiola Sepulveda, *Art Director*

Image Credits: p.8 Alamy/PSF Collection; p.9 (top) Library of Congress [LOC-LC-USZ62-106674]; p.14 (top) USGS; p.14 (left) Library of Congress LC-USZ62-11808; p.15 (top) Alamy/North Wind Picture Archives; p.15 (bottom) Library of Congress [LC-USZ62-20270]; p.16 (top left) Alamy; p.16 (right) Library of Congress [LOC LC-USZ62-112234]; p.16 (middle left) Getty Images/Graphic House; p.17 (middle) Alamy/Shiiko Alexander; p.17 (bottom) Library of Congress [LC-USZ62-88309-hopi]; p.18 Alamy/US Marines Photo; p.19 (left) Wikimedia/James, George Wharton; p.19 (right) Alamy/Natural History Archive; p.21 (top) Library of Congress [LOC LC-USZ62-112673]; p.23 (bottom) National Park Service; all other images from iStock and/or Shutterstock

This book has been filed with the Library of Congress.
LCCN: 2026018288
ISBN: 979-8-3309-2993-1

TCM Teacher Created Materials
5482 Argosy Avenue
Huntington Beach, CA 92649
www.tcmpub.com

Printed by 51250
PO 22957 / Printed in USA

Table of Contents

Why Do People Visit and Protect Landmarks?

Landmarks are like the world's show-and-tell. They're the places that make people stop, look, and say, "**Wow!**"

Some landmarks were shaped by nature. Others were built by people.

People visit landmarks to learn, explore, and feel inspired. They remind us of what's special about our **environment** and why it's worth taking care of. When we protect landmarks, we make sure that future generations can stand in those same amazing places and say, "Wow!" too.

Here are four **popular** landmarks. Can you name the ones that are **natural** and the ones that are made by people?

Natural Bridge in Utah

Statue of Liberty in New York

A Landmark That Grows!

When the sun warms the Eiffel Tower, its metal expands. So, it grows a little taller! As it cools, the tower shrinks back down.

Eiffel Tower in France

What makes the Grand Canyon so remarkable?

Let's find out!

Grand Canyon in Arizona

A True Natural Wonder

The Grand Canyon is one of the most amazing places on Earth! You can find it at the Grand Canyon National Park in northern Arizona.

This giant canyon is very special. It's even been named one of the Seven Natural Wonders of the World. People have lived here for thousands of years. The Havasupai peoples still call it home.

The canyon is full of life. You might spot cacti and tall trees, soaring eagles, or sure-footed bighorn sheep. The pink **rattlesnake** lives *only* in the Grand Canyon area.

When the sun hits the canyon walls, they glow with shades of **red**, **orange**, and **gold**. The cliffs and rocks that have been carved over centuries look like towers and castles. It's easy to see why people call this place a wonder!

Road Trip!

The canyon is 277 miles (446 kilometers) long. That's more than the drive from New York City to Washington, DC!

Over millions of years, layers of sand, mud, and rock built up on top of each other.

Pieces of sand and rock called **sediment** wash away. Erosion and gravity pull sand and rocks down, changing the canyon's shape.

Rain, snow, ice, and wind keep **eroding** the canyon. In winter, water freezes in cracks, and in spring it thaws, making the cracks grow. The growing cracks chip away the rocks.

The Colorado River slowly carved through the rock to make the canyon.

Layers of History

The Grand Canyon has layers and layers of rock, stacked like pages in a history book. Each layer tells a story of how the land changed over millions of years. Long ago, this land was lifted high by powerful forces deep within the earth. Then, the Colorado River began to flow. It slowly carved its way through the rising rock. Over time, wind, water, and ice helped shape the steep cliffs and wide valleys we see today. The deeper the canyon goes, the older and more **colorful** the rock layers become.

The Grand Canyon Through Time

The Grand Canyon's story began millions of years ago. From rushing rivers to busy park trails, it has changed again and again. Take a look at how this amazing place has changed through time.

Many American Indians, including the Havasupai, Hopi, Zuni, and Navajo, make their homes here.

thousands of years ago

6 million years ago

The Colorado River begins carving its way through ancient layers of rock.

1860s

Explorers and mapmakers begin sharing the canyon's beauty with the world.

1880s

The first hotels open, welcoming travelers to see the canyon's amazing views.

1901

The Grand Canyon Railway begins carrying visitors to the South Rim.

1919

The Grand Canyon becomes a national park, protecting it for everyone to enjoy.

today

Millions of people visit Grand Canyon National Park every year.

Amazing Sights and How to See Them

Every year, about five million people visit the Grand Canyon. It's easy to see why!

The South Rim is the most popular spot. From here, you can walk right up to the edge and look out for **miles and miles.** The view will take your breath away!

The **Bright Angel Trail** starts at the South Rim. It's a tough walk heading toward the Colorado River, but the hike back up is the real challenge.

Colorado River

After about 4.5 miles (7.24 kilometers), you'll reach **Havasupai Gardens**. It's a shady resting area with trees and cool, flowing water.

If you keep going another 1.5 miles (2.4 kilometers), you'll come to **Plateau Point**. Here you'll see views of the sparkling Colorado River far below.

Bright Angel Trail

Start here

Beware of "Friendly" Rock Squirrels!

These cute, little creatures come right up to tourists. But be careful. Sometimes, they bite!

The Skywalk is a bridge made of glass. It stretches 70 feet (21 meters) out from the edge of the canyon! When you look through the glass floor, you can see 3,600 feet (1.1 kilometers) straight below. It looks like you're walking on air!

If you're up for a thrill, try rafting on the Colorado River. The **rapids** make an exciting ride. At night, rafters camp on sandy river beaches under the light of thousands of stars.

For a big-screen adventure, visit the Grand Canyon IMAX Theater in the nearby town of Tusayan. The movie takes you deep into the canyon. You'll *fly* over cliffs, *race* down the river, and meet wildlife up close—all while learning the canyon's amazing history.

Will the Glass Break?

The Skywalk can hold 71 million pounds. That's like 71 large planes filled with people.

Mapping the Grand Canyon

Long ago, the Grand Canyon was a mystery to much of the world. In 1869, explorer and scientist John Wesley Powell led a daring expedition. He and his small team traveled hundreds of miles through the canyon in wooden boats. They faced roaring rapids, steep cliffs, and powerful storms. But they also managed to make the first known map of the Grand Canyon! Powell's map helped the world see how big and awe-inspiring the Grand Canyon really is.

John Wesley Powell

The first expedition lasted approximately 3 months!

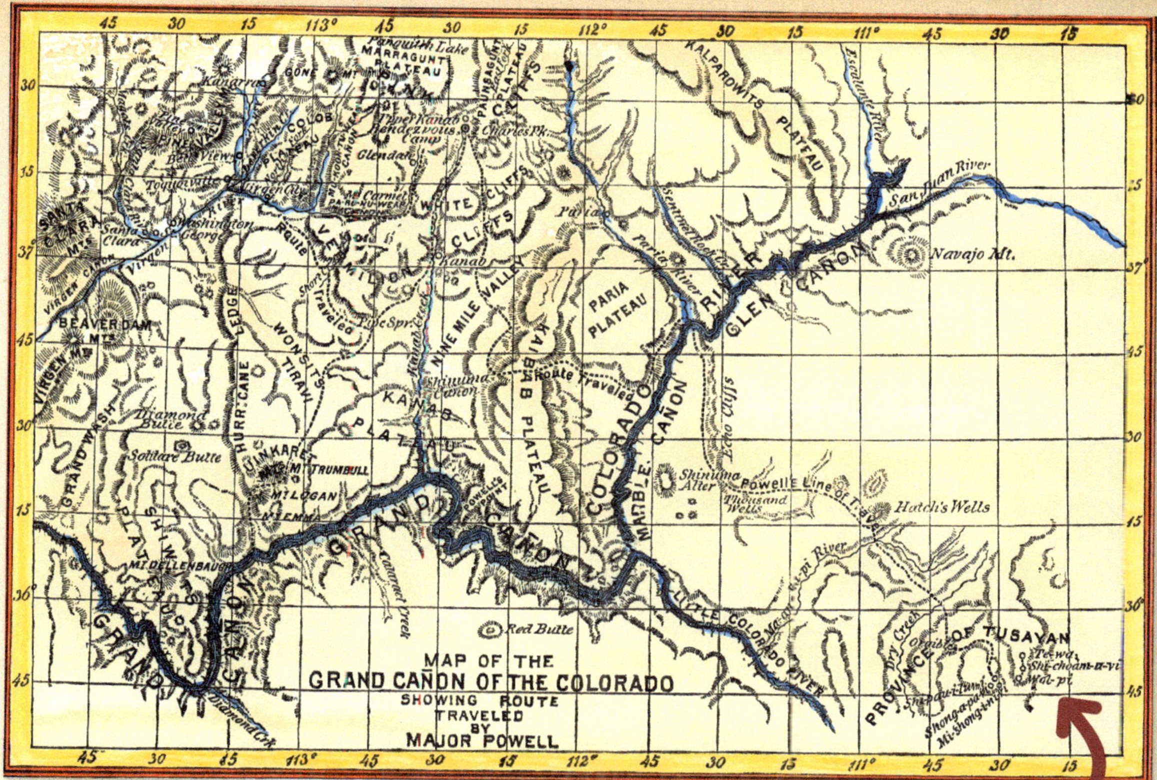

This map of the Grand Canyon was drawn by Powell in the 1870s.

Stories of the Canyon

The Grand Canyon is a sacred and special place for many **tribal** nations. It's like a giant storybook carved in stone. Long ago, the canyon gave people food, water, and shelter. Many made their homes along its cliffs and rivers.

Even today, people of the nations share their stories about this awe-inspiring place. The Hopi say it's where their people first came into the world. The Zuni believe their spirits travel here when they die. The Navajo tell stories of holy people who shaped parts of the canyon itself.

The Grand Canyon is so much more than layers of rock. It's a place filled with life, history, and stories that live on.

Oral Tradition

Many people pass down stories by telling them out loud. One generation tells the next. This is known as *oral* ***tradition***.

Elderly members of the Havasupai tribe rest on a bench in their tribal homeland at the bottom of the Grand Canyon.

One nation has called the Grand Canyon home for at least 800 years. They are the Havasupai, which means *people of the blue-green water.*

The Havasupai live in Supai **Village**, tucked deep in the very bottom of the canyon. Their home is near a big, beautiful waterfall. The minerals in the water make it shimmer a bright blue-green color. It looks almost magical.

In the village, there is a school, a post office, a store, and a restaurant. The Havasupai elders work hard to keep their language, stories, and traditions alive. They teach them to each new generation, so their way of life continues to flow—just like the blue-green river.

The Havasupai school, built in 1899, was rebuilt in the 1930s after it was damaged by a flood.

Supai Village

Deep in the base of the Grand Canyon sits **Supai Village**. It is a special place within the vast Grand Canyon.

Did You Know?

The village is so deep in the canyon that you can only get there by foot or pack animal.

The Havasupai people have lived here for **hundreds of years**!

Havasupai means "**People** of the **Blue-Green Water**."

You can **hike**, ride a **mule**, or fly in a **helicopter** to reach the village.

A Canyon Like No Other

There are many other large canyons in the world, but none quite like the Grand Canyon. Its cliffs glow with colors, like nature picked up a paintbrush and created a masterpiece on stone.

The canyon's size makes it grand, but it's more than that. The Grand Canyon has a story to tell. Every layer holds pieces of history and culture, waiting to be discovered. That's what fills people with awe and wonder every time they visit.

The canyon reminds us that the world is full of mysteries. It invites us to wonder and explore. Each stone and shadow has a story to tell, if only we look and listen.

Stories in Stone

Fossils found in the canyon's walls and caves tell stories of ancient plants and animals that once made it their home.

Around the World

There are many large canyons on our planet. Each one is special in its own way. Some are longer than others, some are deeper, but all are amazing! Let's explore a few other "grand" canyons from around the world.

Yarlung Tsangpo Grand Canyon

Tibet

It is one of the longest and deepest canyons in the world. Snowy mountains and a winding river make it a beautiful sight.

Look Out Below!

If you stood on the rim of the Grand Canyon and dropped a pebble, it would fall for about 20 seconds before hitting the bottom!

Colca Canyon

Peru

This canyon is one of the deepest in the world. It is known for the giant condors that glide above its cliffs. Ancient farms still line its steep walls.

Verdon Gorge

France

It is known for its river with bright blue-green water. It is a favorite place for hiking and kayaking.

Copper Canyon

Mexico

It is actually made of six canyons in a row. Together, they are four times larger than the Grand Canyon.

Fish River Canyon

Namibia

It is 100 miles (160 kilometers) long. It was carved by the river through dry desert land.

Just for You

You don't have to visit the Grand Canyon to explore and care for the world around you. Here are some fun ways to learn, create, and wonder right where you are!

Story Circle

Sit in a circle with family or friends and tell stories of your experiences. What adventures have you had? What are your favorite memories? Take turns telling the stories.

Landmark Walk

Take a walk with a grown-up and look for landmarks near your home. Maybe they are statues, signs, or special buildings. Maybe they are mountains, rocks, or rivers. What stories do they tell?

Snack Rocks

Make a tasty "canyon" snack. Use a clear, glass jar and create layers with treats like pudding, crushed cookies, raisins, crushed graham crackers, and more. The layers look like the Grand Canyon's rocks!

Canyon Detective

Flip through *Our Grand Canyon* again and see how many animals you can find in the text and images.

Nature's Promise

Draw or write one way you can help protect nature. Maybe it is picking up litter, recycling, or sharing what you've learned about the Grand Canyon.

Glossary

environment—the air, water, land, and living things that surround us

eroding—wearing away due to water, wind, or ice

fossils—the remains or shapes of plants or animals that lived long ago, found in rock

landmarks—objects or structures on land that are easy to see or recognize and may be important in history

natural—made by nature

popular—well-liked

rapids—fast-moving parts of a river where the water rushes over rocks

sediment—loose material such as dirt, sand, and pebbles that is deposited by water, wind, or ice

tradition—a belief or custom that is handed down to younger family members

tribal—related to a group of people who share language and culture

village—a very small town

Index

Be Curious

1. How was the Grand Canyon formed?
2. What plants and animals live in the Grand Canyon?
3. How have people used and valued the Grand Canyon through history?
4. What can we do to help protect the Grand Canyon for the future?

About the Author

Jennifer Prior lives about an hour's drive from the Grand Canyon. She has visited it on multiple occasions. At age 13, her family camped in the national park for a week. She spent hours looking at the canyon from different sites, imagining all the things within its walls. Since then, she has hiked to Havasupai Falls several times. As a professor at Northern Arizona University, she hiked to Supai Village with groups of education students, hosting literacy festivals for the elementary school. She and her husband live in Flagstaff, Arizona, with their dog, Monica, and cats, Mary and Chad.